WAKING AND ALWAYS

Poetry
HOMECOMING
A BALL OF GOLD: POEMS FOR CHILDREN
COUNTERPOISE
WINDFALLS

Non-fiction
BLATANT AND PROUD

Fiction
THE BOWGADA BIRDS AND OTHER STORIES

WAKING AND ALWAYS

Poems by Andrew Lansdown

ANGUS
& ROBERTSON
PUBLISHERS

Creative writing programme assisted by the Literature Board of the Australia Council, the Federal Government's arts funding and advisory body.

ANGUS & ROBERTSON PUBLISHERS

Unit 4, Eden Park, 31 Waterloo Road, North Ryde, NSW, Australia 2113, and 16 Golden Square, London WIR 4BN, United Kingdom

First published in Australia by Angus & Robertson Publishers in 1987

National Library of Australia Cataloguing-in-publication data.

Lansdown, Andrew, 1954– .
Waking and always: poems.
ISBN 0 207 15530 5.

I. Title.

A821'.3

Typset in 10 pt English Times
Printed in Singapore

For Zenon Pirga
and Peter Good

the garment of praise for the spirit of heaviness
Isaiah, lxi:iii

Acknowledgements

Poems in this collection (some in slightly different form) have previously appeared in the *Age*, *An Inflection of Silence and Other Poems* (University of Newcastle, 1986), *Australian*, *Christians Writing*, *Fremantle Arts Review*, *Instructions for Honey Ants and Other Poems* (University of Newcastle, 1983), *Linq*, *Northern Perspective, On Being*, *Overland*, *Patterns*, *Poem of Thanksgiving and Other Poems* (University of Newcastle, 1985), *Poems Selected from the Australian's 20th Anniversary Competition* (Angus & Robertson, 1985), *Poetry Australia*, *Portrait: a West Coast Collection* (Fremantle Arts Centre Press, 1986), *Quadrant*, *Southerly*, *Southern Review*, *The Angus and Robertson Book of Australian Light Verse* (1987), *This Australia, Westerly* and *Windfalls* (Fremantle Arts Centre Press, 1984).

Some poems have been broadcast on *A First Hearing* (Australian Broadcasting Corporation) and *Writers' Radio* (Radio 5UV, University of Adelaide).

The author gratefully acknowledges financial assistance (to write some of the "river" poems) from Ian Burton, Peter Kelly and Russell Smith.

The author gratefully acknowledges financial assistance from the Literature Board of the Australia Council.

Contents

The Horseshoe Shooter	1
Poised on a Premonition	2
The *Shodō* Egret	3
Choka for Sacred Kingfisher	5
New Leaf	6
Casuarina, Walyunga	7
Poem about Freedom	9
Daystar	10
Tenant	11
For Susan (1)	12
Absence	13
Goshawk	14
Bird Haiku	15
On Haiku	16
A Remembrance of Robins	17
Birds, South Perth Zoo	18
Cat	19
This Place	20
Zoo Vignettes	22
Green Elephants	23
Images	24
Farm Haiku	25
Rabbits	26
Kangaroos Crossing	27
The Swift Stone	28
Rapids, Upper Swan	29
Duck and Wake	30
Ford	31
Snake	32
In Prison	33
For Fear of Freedom	34
Confinement	35
Waiting to Greet Me	36
Sharing a Joke	37
Stepping Out	38
Far from Home, the Blower	39
Waiting, Singing	42

Wind	43
Pigeons	44
Water Tank	45
Slaters in Grass	46
Spring Morning with Baby and Birds	47
Haiku for Susan	48
Distortions	49
The Thing Signified	50
Should I Fall and Fail to Rise	51
Dance	54
Lighting a Match	55
By Stone and Water	56
For Susan (2)	57
In Transit	58
For Grace	60
She Enters with Flowers	61
Mint	62
While Watering Vegetables	63
September	64
Petal Poem	65
Tree and Tank	66
Moth in Rain	67
Snake in a Box	68
Intentions	69
Circles	70
Fly in a Flagon	71
Frightening Father	72
The Commune Worker's Communique	73
People in Zoos	74
Haiku: Fremantle Harbour	75
Wind on Canvas	76
Decussation	77
Ford and Trees	78
Straw-necked Ibises	79
Snake with Angel	80
Not in Truce	81
Waking and Always	82

The Horseshoe Shooter

It is almost dark. A car passes
without its lights on. My son shoots it
with the hook end of his hockey stick.
"It shoots horseshoes," he says.
I imagine a horseshoe
lobbing neatly onto the peg of the driver's neck.
"Piaow! Piaow!" cries my daughter,
improvising with her finger.
"Was this yours?" The old stick
is a new gift from his grandparents.
"No," I say. "It was my brother's."
"Uncle David's?" My daughter is merely
revising the relationships: dad's brother, my uncle.
"No. My brother Stephen. He's dead."
They are both suddenly quiet. Their father
has a brother who is dead. Our father.
"Did you have any other brothers?"
"Yes. Philip." "Is he dead?" "Yes."
The horseshoe shooter has become a music stick
piping death from the basket of my life.
It rises up, the old snake, flicks
its forked tongue, flares its hood, sways, holds
them mesmerised. "Were you grown up?"
They are thinking of each other now,
these little children, my son and daughter,
brother and sister. If dad was a boy when ...
are *we* safe? "Yes," I say.
Well, almost. "Yes, I was grown up."
They are relieved. But my daughter asks,
"And are you the oldest?"
"Well, I am now." "Good," she says,
as if all uncertainties were now
settled, as if night were now the only darkness
coming upon the world. "Good."

Poised on a Premonition

I sit waiting for a fish
to telegraph its presence to my fingers.
There is no communication.
Are there fish in the depths? Perhaps
they are poised on a premonition
of death. My son jerks his line,
imitating the old men at the end
of the jetty. My little daughter,
resenting her mother's restraining hand,
dangles a stone-weighted stocking
into the water. From the far side of the estuary,
the kek-kek cry of a kestrel
fires at us. What, I wonder, has it killed?

"I've got one, dad!" Clumsily,
he pulls in his line: a small bream
whirls against its will
upward to the suffocating air—
its life a thread of silver, unravelling
through the clear water.
It is small; but my son will not spare it.
As it dries and dies on the jetty,
a faint, rainbowing iridescence
disappears from its head.

I feel a bite, bring in a trumpet fish.
It hangs from my line like a chime
fluttering in the winds of death.
It trumpets softly, as if crooning endearments,
as I jiggle the hook from its mouth.
I hold it to my daughter's ear.
"He's talking to me." She turns to touch
its eye. "He likes me, doesn't he, dad?"

The *Shodō* Egret

Engrossed, the egret
on the shore neglects
the glint of whitebait
in the sheet water

at its feet. It does not
note its reflection
needled like a tattoo
on the river's skin,

nor reflect that it
can lie as lightly
on air as an image
on liquid. Today,

fish are no food, light
no enlightenment,
flight no fancy. It seeks
another excellence.

In *shodō,* the Way
of Writing, the egret
pursues perfection.
Each measured footfall

is a meditation
in calligraphy.
Each delicate foot
is three *hosofude*,

slender brushes; and
each step is three
brushstrokes, converging
on a common point,

pointing to a past
step towards this step.
The white sand is rice
paper; and the bird

prints it repeatedly,
striving to perfect
its character. Egret—
master of spear,

subject of painting
and poetry—only
calligraphy is
lacking for inner

nobility. Now
it stands on one leg
as if poised, focused
for a final effort—

places with precision
its tri-tufted brush
through the still water.
Lifting up, it leaves,

as if beneath glass,
exquisitely, al-
most excellently,
its pristine figure.

Almost. Such sadness—
to know perfection, yet
never to reach it.
Croaking a regret

it flies to the sun,
the *shodō* egret.

Choka for Sacred Kingfisher

If I draw too close
it flies away. Otherwise
it appears not to
notice me at all: the small
kingfisher that comes
to my garden at nightfall
and sets me fishing
for image and metaphor.
It is a brush-stroke
of blue, framed among apples,
famed among feathers.
Still against the shifting leaves,
motionless, it dives
deep into the pools of praise
and surfaces with
itself, conveys nothing else.
It shapes the sprawling
tree by reference to itself:
a sharp cynosure.
Without knowledge of self, it
enacts itself precisely.

New Leaf

Spiking from the centre of the older leaves,
extending the line of the trunk
straight up like a green lightning rod
or, later as it loosens, like a rolled newspaper
flaring at the free end: the new banana leaf.
When unfurled, it is unbroken
but lined, as a coupon for tearing.
Newly open, bending slightly
towards the inevitable earth, it is
broad and smooth: a lacquered ceremonial paddle;
an elongated elephant's ear. Then too soon
the wind tugs and teases it,
tears it to tatters until it flutters
shabbily, like a string of streamers at a car yard.

Casuarina, Walyunga

The tree by the river
is a casuarina, a she-oak that rises
from a reticulation of exposed roots
fanning like rivulets over the flatland
that dries in summer to a mere dampness.

The tree by the river
is a river of wood
pouring into the air
through a tangle of tributaries.

It is a spider
spinning a wooden web
over the black clay
to catch the beetle-backed stones.

It is a dark place
that dugites are slithering into.

The tree by the river
is a vertical glacier
upheld by a horizontal delta.

It is a congealed artery
clotted to a network of varicose veins.

It is a giant nerve
synapsed to the earth.

It is an enormous amoeba
flowing into pseudopods.

The tree by the river
is an axle
radiating bent, bifurcating spokes.

It is the south pole
drawing longitudinal lines
that wobble into latitude.

It is a conductor rod
struck at the base by forked lightning.

It is a powerhouse
feeding sunlight to the earth
through a gridwork of cables.

The tree by the river
is a cartographer
charting the concentric
contour lines of the land.

It is a conservationist
enmeshing the soil
against the eroding water.

It is a constructionist
scaffolding the ground for renovations.

The tree by the river
is a fisherman
casting a circular net
on a site where minnows will swim in winter.

It is a tribal elder
renewing the rituals of initiation,
cicatrising the chest of the black earth.

It is the Rainbow Serpent
giving birth to thin black snakes.

The tree by the river
is a lubra
knotting her slender toes to the earth,
lifting her supple arms to the wind.
She is weeping, tossing her hair and
wailing for the warriors
whose bones lie in the red loam
not far from the running water,
the young warriors
who will never return to Walyunga.

Poem about Freedom

I am sitting in the shade
of the lemon tree, trying to write
a poem about freedom. But

my son is swinging in the almond,
calling, "Dad, look at this! Dad!"
The day conspires to distract me

from things I have designated
important. On a branch
arching over me, a lemon's

green rind is yielding to yellow.
Near my feet, a hornet
is hurtling sand from a hole

set in a clear space
between the rootbound and budless
chrysanthemums. In the apple tree

the fruit's round cheeks
are powdered with rouge
and a parrot is summoning its mate

to a feast. Now my daughter
crams her rag doll
in the cane chair beside me and

places in its lap a sprig of mint.
Bruised by her clumsy hands
it smells so clean and sweet.

Daystar

The almond tree I meant to cut down last autumn
has leaves again. And this but mid-winter!
At the tip of one twig, tilted to face my window,
a single flower has battled through the bark.
Doubtless, it will unfasten without fruit; but
it sets in the graft of my imagination
like a star, a daystar unneedful of the dark.

Tenant

Lifting a brick, I make
an oblong room
walled by weeds
chandeliered by seeds
of wild oats. And

on the floor
of this unroofed house,
curled like a peeled
bonsai mandarin,
there is a wood louse.

For Susan (1)

I am won and wounded by
the apparition of the apple tree
beneath the black sky:

a thousand leaves shifting
singularly in the one wind,
and the white petals sifting

to the dark and dunged loam.
Tell me, lady—in my absence
has our apple come into bloom?

And have the petals fallen to your hair
as once last summer
I saw them fall and snare?

Absence

And daddy, you know what?
I'm a bit lonely about you.

From 3,000 miles away,
her voice so sweet and clear.

Goshawk

Birds burst from the almond tree.
And looking up I see a goshawk
standing on a branch. Its head
ratchets on its shoulders, yellow eyes
unblinking. It fluffs its feathers,
looks suddenly lighter, bigger—
a bird leavened by blood
in the heart of winter.
It lifts one leg, tucks it
beneath the coverlet of feathers; and then
snugs the quill-quilt to the body's bed.
As if a hand had brushed its breast
it is again sharp and sleek. The goshawk,
one-taloned and doveless in the leafless tree.

Bird Haiku

i
An axe in the red
split wood. On the grey handle
a fantail alights.

ii
Thornbills, dull and grey,
flit across the field, yellow
flashing from their rumps.

iii
Chattering scallywag
on the ridge of the cow's rump:
the small Willie Wag.

iv
A dusting of white
ash stirs on the bright coals as
the robin alights.

On Haiku

Haiku are pebbles
poets lob into the pond
of our emotions.

A Remembrance of Robins

From the twig where they rested
I saw them flit away: two robins
white-capped and scarlet-breasted.

And for a moment they invested
the countryside with colour
from the twig where they rested.

No flower, no other bird contested
the bright display of these two—both
white-capped and scarlet-breasted.

Without warrant they arrested
me: plum blossoms seemed to bloom
from the twig where they rested.

And in departure they divested
the bush of brightness: bobbing away, robins
white-capped and scarlet-breasted.

Birds, South Perth Zoo

i
Black foot in the white back feathers,
the floating swan,
conserving heat by contortion.

ii
As if to strengthen the sockets,
yellow ring reinforcements
around the pelican's eyes.

iii
By the stones, no stone
curlew in the cage.

iv
Picking up precisely
as with tongs
a single grain of wheat
and tossing it back
into the throat:
the white ibis.

v
Brolga, Native Companion,
stately
under the circumstances.

Cat

A stray cat has just
eaten a fragment of cheese
my daughter dropped from
her plate and left lying on
the back lawn where we
lunched two hours ago—and now
it is climbing on
to the chair where she sat and
is eskimo-kissing,
gingerly sniffing the weathered
canvas, testing tent-
atively with whisker and
paw the pliable
surface, wondering I suppose
(I could say for sure
if this poem would wait—and now
two weeks later it still won't
wait) if the chair is
a good place to curl up and
nap in the weak winter sun.

This Place

Sticking to the side
of the rusted incinerator,
a small skink—

and below it, snarled
among weeds, tender
for fire, a tinder

of rose-clippings.
This place is death
little lizard.

With a delicacy and precision
to surpass all imagery,
it glances at me

cocking its head like a dog.
This place is death.
Gingerly, I reach out . . . but

it darts towards the ashes,
disappears among the thorns
and dry grasses.

I poke about, impatient
for fire. But the skink
does not think of flame or smoke.

It will not come out.
Who am I
to have the care of every creature

in my hand? If I had not seen . . .
I drop a lighted match
into the drum.

This place is my place
and my place is death
little lizard.

I do not wait to watch
the refuse fragment with flame.
But, hauntingly, a hymn

takes me in its hum:
His eye is on the sparrow
and I know He watches me.

Zoo Vignettes

i
In the confined water,
seals—torpedoes
fired at no target.

ii
Gibbon—arms like chewing gum.
Voice sort of stretchy, too.

iii
On the roof of the empty cage,
crested pigeons, preening.

iv
Smaller than a rabbit's,
the giraffe's droppings.

v
An Indian mynah, singing
on the camel's hump.

vi
In the platypus aquarium,
only the husks of yabbies.

vii
On the flank of the tiger snake,
the yellow scales,
hexagonal, like honeycomb.

viii
Chimpishly, the chimps:
today as yesterday
quite untroubled by questions
of captivity or ancestry.

ix
The carpet squares
on the bull giraffe's neck
are threadbare, faded.
On the fur, evidence
of itching or entropy?

Green Elephants

The Abyssinian banana trees
in the zoological gardens: surely
they are a herd of elephants
standing on great unbending legs.

And see how here and there a new leaf—
laminae freshly unfolded,
petiole and midrib uplifted—
is a trunk held in salute,

draped ceremonially in emerald cloth.

Images

i
Like a shred of cirrus,
the black-shouldered kite
is cuffed from its pivot-point
by the cat-pawed wind.

ii
As I walk in the pastured hills,
shadows of clouds
move about me like cows.

Farm Haiku

i
Mingling with the sheep,
a murder of crows straggle
through the grey stubble.

ii
Into the dam's mould
the late afternoon sun is
pouring molten gold.

iii
Dusk. By the dam's edge,
herons, stabbing little fish
in the failing light.

Rabbits

A bobbing of white
signals their presence: rabbits,
stump-grey in twilight

sitting at the edge
of the green paddock, beneath
the lantana hedge.

Kangaroos Crossing

Emerging from Boongarup Pool
the river flows through
an arbour of casuarinas
then widens to a ford
cobbled with round stones.

On the alluvial flats
beside the broad shallows
I disturbed three kangaroos
from their dozing. Startled,
they fled across the ford,

startling in turn a statue
that broke into a bird.
Now they're gone I see them
again: kangaroos bounding
through the troubled water

and a heron flying up.

The Swift Stone

The swift stone
in the still river
is a motor boat
churning a wake
of white water.

Rapids, Upper Swan

The rocks in the river
are repeatedly breaking
the sheet-glassed water.
See the white shards
spinning away!

Duck and Wake

Behind the swimming duck
but between the wake's V
the water's skin crimples,
dimples like simmering milk.

Ford

The stones are salmon
swimming up the shallows, water
skidding off their backs.

Snake

The same as with men,
only less dangerously

the dugite

where the head goes
the body follows

In Prison

At least in here,
she said, *he*

can't get at me
or make me do

something
I don't want to.

For Fear of Freedom

She has mutilated, humiliated
herself again, the young woman
soon to be released. Who can help
someone so lonely, so unlovely?
Everywhere she goes, everyone
ignores her injuries. As when
she vandalised the cupboards
but was not charged, this self
disfigurement is futile.
For no matter what
she does, they will send her out.
Even here, no one wants her.

Confinement

On the oblong of lawn
between the barred
walkway and the wall,
the young Malaysian woman

straw hat held
against the slight wind,
free arm extended
for balance

steps
sideways to avoid
the sprinkler's spray
in the confined space

lifts
astonishingly her feet
like an Andalusian horse
dancing.

Waiting to Greet Me

He tends the garden strip
on freedom's side of the wall.
After 7 years, obedience
is his confinement. They call him
a Trusty. "Freedom
in four weeks," he tells me,
his smile as open
as his security rating.

Four weeks. And one day
I arrived at his absence.
Four weeks, and he is gone.

Some mornings now, if
I'm off-guard, I find myself
wishing he were still here,
green-uniformed among the shrubbery,
waiting to greet me.

Sharing a Joke

We are standing in the prison
art room. *She was about to say sorry*
he says, stepping back
from his painting of purple genitalia
like bougainvillaea blossom
incidentally fastened to a woman
withering into the background,
when I shot her.
She was on her knees:
"*Oh! Oh! Please* . . ."
Now he is kneeling, laughing,
this man some view as a victim.
And another man is laughing with him.
They feel at ease with me,
treat me as an honorary crim.
I value their acceptance. But knowing
how easily brotherhood inspires betrayal
I turn away, unwilling even to grin.

Stepping Out

Stepping out, the last gate
locking me into freedom,
I hear the sweet chatter of parrots
as they break the red berries
in the cotoneaster bush
by the convict-built wall.

Far from Home, the Blower

Close off one end of the didgeridoo
and look down the other—
that's how black he is, this Kimberley man.
He has come to the school for the didgeridoo.
He wants to take it back to his cell;
but I cannot give him permission
immediately. This is a maximum security prison:
procedures must be observed. So
he is playing it now in the literacy room.
I tell the officers he will be staying
for the afternoon. He is playing it now.
His eyes are closed and he is tapping
the plastic seat with his thumb-nail
as the pipe drones at his feet.
Abruptly, in a gesture of harmony,
he breaks his rhythm. *That lillgah*
he says. I do not understand.
Lillgah, he says, slowly, several times.
I cannot get it right. *Lillgah—like tuning.*
Making didgeridoo same as singer.
He plays again. A singer silent to me
is chanting in the channels of his ear.
He listens, trying to match his music
to the key and rhythm of the voice.
We always do this, start
with lillgah. If the singer not happy
with one blower, he get another.
Me a deep blower. He blows again. Indeed
the drone is deep. But I never knew
it could be otherwise. *Some singers are high.*
You know? Clear. He throws his head back,
taps his throat. And he sings—high, nasally,
rhythmic, in "language".
I know this singing, but its meaning
is ancient and alien. He is singing
and we are in harmony. I do not
ask for meanings. But I say,
Sing low then, Simon. And he sings
low and husky, unlike anything
I have heard before. *The blower*

must be the same. See?
He plays again. A different rhythm.
An officer comes in, jangling
his keys. O freedom! I do not look up.
The didgeridoo drones vibrantly,
striking up a resonance in my soul.
Taut or slack, spiritual chords
are strung across the hollow
at the heart of every man.
No man is mere matter—therefore
the Dreaming. "Kudda, brother,"
one of the tribal men from Kalgoorlie way
calls me. A man from Noonkanbah Station
greets me behind these walls as "Papaji,
brother." Simon does not call me "brother";
but he is playing the didgeridoo
for me. He breaks off suddenly. *Now*
the young girls come in. Jdirree-jdirree.
He flicks his hands, makes a few staccato
movements with his torso. *Wanga.*
That the Law. The women start first.
He begins again, the familiar droning
tempered by new rhythms and sounds.
And somewhere in the didgeridoo
a brolga begins to dance and cry.
The men this time. First the brolga
dance. He stops again. *Now*
a dingo. She crying for her pup. And
distant through the droning, a dingo
barks and howls in the hollow
of the didgeridoo. *When I was initiated* . . .
He is rehearsing his life.
And I am like a cut and ochred
hollow branch: he speaks into me
evoking a sympathy that, in turn, stirs
his heart to a symphony of longing.
When I am made a man, the blower
he's playing all day. Never stop.
He be giving me his wind.
And they give me a didgeridoo, to be
a blower. But I never play
all day for initiation. I never be picked
to play all night for corroboree.
I only play short time. For fun.

You know? Maybe for white people too.
For fun. Like frogs. Gningi-gningi.
I can't catch the words.
He is sharing unfamiliar things
in a voice too quiet and quick. *A good blower,*
he cut his tongue with spinifex.
He pokes out his tongue. It is very pink
against his purple lips. He runs his thumb-nail
down the tip. Yours cut? I ask.
No. Too fat. But good blower
he listens. He hears. He gets the wisdom of it.
He cuts his tongue, gets plenty sounds.
Plenty wind. Like tortoise. Like crocodile.
You know? His gaze is distant.
He is dreaming. *To be a blower*,
he says, *to be a didgeridoo-man*
is good. You know? Get respect. Get proudness.

Waiting, Singing

She is past eighty and past impatience,
the woman waiting, singing,
by my writing room window
at the Old Age Centre. She is waiting
for her middle-aged son
who will come, as usual, at his leisure.
And she is singing—sitting on a bench
on the open verandah in the late
mid-winter afternoon—singing—
a tuneless *la-la*-ing
from the shrivelled mouth, the shining heart.
It angers me, his neglect.
Do I conjecture unjustly? Yet truly!
daily, after the Centre is deserted,
she is left waiting, companioned alone
by a voice unmatched to her memories of music.
It disconcerts me, her docility.
So little time left.
Such a waste, just waiting.
Or is it? Perhaps it is glorious
to be singing and not resenting
time going or death coming.

Wind

The wind, that robust roustabout,
has flung a flocculence of cloud
across the grading table of the sky.

Pigeons

Below the cloud bank, a flock of pigeons
wheels in a sudden wash of sunlight, glints
like whitebait shying in the shallows.

Water Tank

The rain tank by the banana trees:
tap it, follow the corrugations down
until the knuckle's knock
is muffled by water. Climb up,
slide the hatch half-off, find
floating in the blackness
a half-moon full of images:
a tuft of cirrus
fathomed in the tank's troposphere;
the underbelly of a banana leaf
its ribbons fluttering upward
like water-weed; and a face
back-lit, looking back at you.
Unbidden, these blessings of light
long hidden in this dark place.

Slaters in Grass

A splicing of shadows and yellows
is the forest of wild oats.

And between the tall trunks
several wood lice, slaters

forage about in their armoured coats
like miniature armadillos.

Spring Morning with Baby and Birds

The sun insinuates brightness through the venetian blind.
Why isn't it raining outside? Birds are choking
with song. Why isn't there silence? Our baby
is on her back in the bassinet, blowing spit
onto her chin. She froths at the mouth like a crab
in a bucket. Seeing me, she rubs her heels together,
staccato, quick. Click! Click! "Go on, little cricket!"
My voice is mechanical, but she smiles just the same.
Her eyes hurt me—so bright with hope. I look away.
She makes a soft sound—the first sound,
apart from crying, of her life—a sort of cooing.
There is a dove in her throat. It becomes in my heart
a bird in a wicker basket. What is this wickedness,
this ingratitude? I place a finger in her palm.
It closes, clasping like a sea anemone.
When she was born, she was embalmed
with vernix. I touched it—a lotion
fit for the thighs of princesses. The old midwives
used to rob the newborn, rub the birth-lotion
on their own bodies. Softer than women, smoother than vernix,
is my daughter's hand. But I am hardened to softness
today. She is trembling with anticipation. But
I do not pick her up—do not
open up to joy. There is a bird in my heart,
fretting. And if it could fly, God would strike it
from the sky. Yet truly, my daughter's smiles,
the spring light, the honeyeaters chirruping
are a burden to me. I prod her.
She coughs out a giggle. In the next room
my other children bicker like politicians.

Haiku for Susan

i
Confetti on wood
and wind and earth: spring and tree
wedded with petals.

ii
Flushed with pink, the white
petals—like your face, lady,
after loving me.

Distortions

And when you look through
the smoke, it makes things look funny,
like they shouldn't look,
said my son, looking through the smoke
of the branches we were burning.

The Thing Signified

"See the swallows?
They look like midgies,
don't they?"

If the thing signified is denied,
what scope is there for comparisons?

"Midgies are bigger than that."
Ignorant of perspective, my son
invents his own scales.

They are indeed small in the distance,
the welcome swallows.

A pelican glides overhead,
big-bodied like a zeppelin.

He does not know "zeppelin".

"Look," I say, pointing.

"A pelican." He knows the bird
and its name.

From across the river,
the *kek-kek* of a kestrel.

"Hear that?"

He listens. "Yes."

"That's a kestrel."

"What d'you mean?"

Would you believe this poem is mine
if you did not know my name?

Should I Fall and Fail to Rise

i
Early in the morning,
before the wind takes up its broom,
you can see where claws
have carved cuneiform runes
into the curve and crest
of the dunes.

Sandcrabs, secretive in sunlight,
solaced by sand,
scavenge the beach by starlight.

Had I the courage, I would come
alone in the dark
to watch their mechanical rituals.

ii
Above the wet sand, there are holes
asterisked by claws.
Creatures governed by laws

as eldritch and rich as the sea,
laws they neither know nor need to learn,
hide in the dark, spurn

both sunlight and me.
I finger a tunnel, scoop the sand
gingerly with my endoskeletal hand.

And suddenly, angrily, there
it is—the sandcrab!
boxbodied like a hansom cab.

iii
High on the beach, the exoskeleton
of a blue manna crab.
Its crablife has crept sideways
into death's sea, leaving
a frail cenotaph
to bleach and crack in the sun.

iv
I gaze at the ocean. Out there
armoured in carapace and claw
roam crabs as long and as hard
as the bones in my arm.

v
Look carefully, and you will see
the shells walk. Hermit crabs
inhabit the reef—housed
in periwinkles and whelks,
tritons and topshells.

And there, in high conical shells,
several crabs waver
with the wash of the water.

Like initiates at a secret ritual,
they dance in their white hats—
the ku klux klansmen
of the crustacean world.

vi
Tiny, translucent-red crabs
hide in the branching coral,
waiting for the debris
of decaying fish.

vii
Camouflaged in combat green
rockcrabs scuttle into crevices.
Waves smash over them, but they remain
immovable. With their periscope eyes
and their bathysphere bodies
they are the ancient world's answer
to science fiction.

viii
Wielding its smallclaw like a broadsword,
holding its shovelclaw like a shield:
the sandcrab. Unless you kill it, it will not yield.

ix

In the sands of the beach
in the rocks by the shore
and on the ocean's floor
crabs click in crustacean speech.

As I walk this beach alone
I begin to realise
should I fall and fail to rise
they will whittle me to the bone.

Dance

Pied cormorants festoon the dead trees
that jut from the steep dunes.
A white egret labours to the air,
croaking protest. On the wooded side
of the river, a sacred kingfisher
glints among the greenery
like a scrap of blue torn from the sky
and blown between the branches.
Fish burst from the startled water
in our wake. An osprey casually pirouettes
onto the stage of my sight. Briefly,
on wind and water, bird and boat
perform a glissading *pas de deux*. Look!
I say, See the bird? Hear the fish?
But my little daughter is lost
in dance. She lilts from side
to side, accentuating the rhythm
of the canoe as I alternate
my weight against the paddle.

Lighting a Match

She has learned at last to strike
the red end on the rough edge.
But still they break mid-stroke
or burn her fingers when they burst
to flame. Each match seems to provoke
a failure, invoke from her a cursed
performance. She has begun to learn
what some Professors profess to spurn:
From literacy to love to lighting a match,
excellence is the objective ledge
onto which each labour must latch.
No charge of "elitism" can hedge
this reality from our sight.
For even small things exact a pledge
that we shall do as they would like.

By Stone and Water

Like a spectre, I am superimposed
over the city. It is not Sydney
I see, but myself, caught in the glass
of the hotel window. I switch off the light,
lose myself in darkness. It is late.
The North Shore scintillates
with innumerable lights. In the black water,
anchored in the bedrock of the harbour,
Pinchgut—where intractable convicts
were crammed and harmed. I imagine myself
out there, bound by stone and water.
In fact, I feel I might as well
be manacled in that fortress
as fret in this room, so far from home.

For Susan (2)

Lady, when we parted
the last petal had drifted
from the almond tree

and the styles were withered
on the foetal fruit
like cut umbilical cords.

They mark my memory:
nuts, nascent, tight
on twig and branch.

Since I left home
have they swollen much?
And our child, is s/he

grown big in your womb?

In Transit

for Mike Kelly

Two deaf women are talking on the train,
their dumb speech dancing
from their hands—an astonishing display

of synaesthesia. On this journey
speech has jettisoned me, finger and tongue.
I am too far from home.

Through the window, briefly, a row
of pines—huge, lopsided, limbs hewn back
from the line, trunks studded with stumps.

In the seat facing mine, a young woman
is asleep. Her head droops from her neck
like a cabbage chrysanthemum on a tall stem.

Her face is hidden, but her hands
are translucent-white, and twitch
like spent moths in the cloth of her lap.

The boomgate's thin bell disturbs her
as we race through a crossing. Her neck stiffens,
lifts the lolling head. But her eyes

remain blanketed in their black beds.
Tiredness is a treason in her body
betraying her to sleep among strangers.

Perhaps she is dying. Indeed
this train is death in transit.
One by one, these people will die.

And so will I. I try not to imagine
the accumulated sorrow crammed
into this railcar. We will grieve

those we love because we live
and must die. Why? And what
does deaf or death matter

if we are mere matter? Uprooted
from the pillaged earth, the pines
stand truncated in my mind;

the young woman still droops and dreams;
the dumb women still speak.
We are strangers before Thee,

hollowed or hallowed by hurt. Father,
the years yield me to yearning
while I tarry in transit to You.

For Grace

Grace is out of grace
for pestering her father.
We are discussing Important Things
and have no time
for praise or prattle or play.
Grace is out of grace.
Forsaking us, she climbs
onto a chest in the bay-window,
rests her face against the pane,
the crocheted curtains
caped about her shoulders.
Outside, an old woman
wavers in her walking to wave
to a child at a window. Grace's hand
flutters up like a sparrow, then falls
still upon the sill as the lady leaves.
Not even a sparrow . . . Father,
may we forever pester You
    for Grace.

She Enters with Flowers

for Liz McKenzie

She enters with flowers, roses
in their European opulence,
pastel-pink and partly open,

and places them in a vase,
a squat stoneware bottle
laying blue in the lacquer

of the dark hardwood table.
Independent of intention, her hands
brush the blooms into a loose

lolling order. This tenderness,
this elegance, elsetimes honoured
as "feminine". Elizabeth.

She enters with flowers,
unsettles the room with roses.
Unable to work, I watch

a white, pin-head spider
parachute from the petals.
Halting mid-air, it hangs

against the crazed face
of the blue-glazed clay,
its cordage caught on a thorn.

Mint

Placing the bucket
by the water tank, I brush
quite by accident
the mint bush. As a bird in
to song, it breaks into scent.

While Watering Vegetables

In the silence of twilight
suddenly there is
a stuttering of white

Cabbage moths,
flushed from hiding,
fluster in the fading light

Of a million things
wonder is also
a winking of wings

They settle again,
havened in my harvest,
until only one remains

Scintillating
above the broad beans

Like the evening star
above the quiet earth

September

I dismissed it yesterday
as a borrowing of yellow
from the broccoli flowers.

But there it is again:
in the bittergreen loquats,
a hint of ripening.

Petal Poem

When the wind flounces the almond tree
petals flurry from the branches
like butterflies caught up in courting.
Exhausted, they spread their wings

on my neighbour's terracotta tiles.
My new neighbour, who felled a red gum
in its frock of white flowers because
it dropped stamens into his gutters.

Tree and Tank

There is a banana tree
by the water tank. And
within the iron reservoir
should you shift
the man-hole hatch,
there is a banana leaf
with its rib and ribbons
lying transversely
on a transparency of light.

Moth in Rain

The moth the colour of kapok
on the windscreen in the rain
is fluttering its wings so fast
they burr like the props of a plane.

Yet try as it will it can't get dry
with the sky opened up like a drain.
Weighted and wet it fans its wings
while the droplets strike it again.

Punch-drunk now from the fragile fists
it sticks to the glass like a stain.

Snake in a Box

Who took a stick to you, snake?
Who smashed the mail
of your hexagonal scales?
Flies sip your eyes, suck
your side—burst
like a sausage on a hot-plate.
Snake, black backed and
yellow bellied, frightening
people to kill you.
Tiger snake, Shere Khan
of the Australian swamps,
why did you leave
your frog and mice
hunting? Just the sight of you
evokes the old enmities—
the bruised head, the wounded
heel—"upon your belly
you shall go". You shall not
go again, poor snake
in a box in the rubbish bin.

Intentions

i
I have to kill the
dragonfly I tried to free
from the spider's web.

ii
Where my axe struck, loose
bark falls away, revealing both
halves of a lizard.

Circles

i
Behind the gauze disc
of the bob-tail's ear, a tick
bulbous with cold blood.

ii
Forming a circle,
the lacewing in the spider's web
bites its blue-tipped tail.

Fly in a Flagon

After throwing a tantrum on its back,
the fly I snatched as it flew
and threw into the flagon unhurt
has accepted quite happily its lot.

Having smoothed its dishevelled wings,
it walks around the glass with (as
my daughter would say) its sticky feet.
Now it's clasping its forefeet with glee,

glad to have escaped the hand of fate.
Foolish, really, such bravado. In fact
those little limbs should lock in prayer.
For already my gecko has spotted it there.

Frightening Father

"Quick! My monster mask!" I said to mum
When I heared dad's key in the lock.
I hided my face so a horrible shock
Would tremble his teeth and wobble his tum.

I crouched on my bed like a leopard on a rock
And bemagined the most cheekiest name to shout.
When dad walked by, I jumped out
And said, "Garr! You dirty old frying sock!"

"Help! A monster!" he cried as he fell on the floor.
I jumped on his back and banged him a boff.
"It's just me, dad!" I said; and I took my mask off
So he wouldn't be frightened no more.

"Oh you sinful singlet! You smouldering smock!
You wicked and worsted waistcoat!" he said;
And he tickled my tummy with his hairy head.
"Mercy!" I said, "You dirty old frying sock!"

The Commune Worker's Communique

A mind like mine is hard to find
In a form like yours—and there's the bind.
Until we met, I'd yet to meet
A woman both of form and feat.

In every way, I think you're neat.
Come swoon on me and be my sweet.
My mud brick hut is warm and snug
And herbal tea awaits your mug.

I'll milk the cow; you'll churn the milk
And spin goat's hair as fine as silk
And bake brown bread and boil brown rice
And cherish treasures beyond price.

We'll gather goodies by the score
From our organic garden store.
We'll live our lives through each impulse
And shun the world and all things false.

I'll stoke your fire in winter's shade;
Nothing we ever do will be staid.
And at the height of summer's heat
I'll draw stream water for your feet.

(Forgive me for the mess I made
Of line eighteen, which ends in "staid".
I know my metre's out of time
But metre had to bow to rhyme.)

I've said enough. Need I say more?
You are the one whom I adore.
Oh lady come, be fierce and fleet!
Shack up with me and be my sweet!

People in Zoos

i
A man clicks his fingers,
a woman waves, but
the oriental otter
stays quite still,
enjoying the performance.

ii
As I did, they are
looking for the thing
signified on the sign
in the empty cage.

iii
In the nocturnal house
you can't help
knocking the glass.

iv
The young woman
leaning to look
at the caged monkeys
is perhaps unaware that

within her loose blouse
her breasts hang
as indolently
as gibbons from a branch.

v
Face to glass to face:
looking at the orang-utan
looking at me.

Haiku: Fremantle Harbour

i
The sunlight patterns
the ship's hull, like the needle
of a seismograph.

ii
Between the wharf and
the ship's hull, thousands of white
jellyfish, pulsing.

Wind on Canvas

All over the bay
aboard sail-boards and yachts
the wind is many women
full and firmly breasted
in triangular-cut bikini tops.

Decussation

Falling by reflection into the river
the tree's two outward-leaning trunks
deflect in the opposite direction.
An exact inversion: V into X:
the forked tree by the still water.

Ford and Trees

Below the confluence of Wooroloo Brook and the Swan
several casuarinas stand in the river, their roots

rising compact and conical above the low water.
A chain downstream, the smooth water widens, drops

as from a ledge, along a row of rounded stones, flows
poppled and scarved with foam over the pebbled shallows.

The casuarina trees are the legs of a draughthorse,
their great hooves tufted, flared with root-hairs.

And the starting stones of the ford are the shares
of a plough, blunt blades of dolerite and granite.

Now see how the horse is drawing the plough
upriver, leaving behind the furrowed water.

See too the kangaroos crossing the long paddock,
their elbowed legs sinking in the loose, white loam.

Straw-necked Ibises

On the grassed river-flats
a flock of ibises—
like elderly orientals
gathered for a festival.

Bald, whiskered, venerable,
they finick over locusts
and other morsels
with their chopstick bills.

Snake with Angel

When it dived, the dabchick, I ran towards
the swamp, wanting to get closer to see better
before the bird surfaced and saw me,
I sprinted towards the swamp, my eyes
on the black hole in the bright-light-green
weed-covered water where the dabchick had dived
and running I was not looking at the ground
I was treading and trod within a fraction
of a snake, a tiger snake, big, black-backed
and lightly banded from the orange belly
by my foot it flicked up
reared up like a jack jarred from its box
sprang up and flattened its head
in fear and fury, flattened its face
like a little-hooded cobra charmed
from its basking by the pipe of my leg
and I staggered off balance like a top
struck while spinning, I stumbled back
expecting through the long seconds
the twin pinholes of poison, oh
expecting, but it teetered, turned, tumbled
down and trickled into the rushes
away from me, and I think (I do not mean
to tread on the snake of your belief
but I must say) I like to think
an angel, my angel, the angel assigned to me
stepped in to stop the snake from striking me.

Not in Truce

Above the black soil of the bulldozed paddock
spiders have spun their threads
on upraised sticks and roots.
In the midst of anarchy, a small affirmation
of design. The webs,
wet with dew and infused with light,
are white pennants raised to proclaim
the mysterious endurance of the powerless.
Or they are bandages of fine gauze,
daubed where limbs have snapped, wrapped
to staunch the flow of beauty from the broken land.

And perhaps it's only little things that will remain
to shore the heart against the broad and brutal ugliness
that looms as the destiny of man. Perhaps
small gestures—the weaving of poems
or the pursuit of a personal integrity
or an unfaltering faith that God is good and
good is no illusion—are all that is left to us.
Like the spiders, we bind the broken roots.
Not in truce, but on trust, we raise
our ragged, regal flags in the winds of a desolate age.

Waking and Always

Naomi, six months

Where has she gone? I do not hold her
as she sleeps in my arms. The tides of air
lift and let go her chest
with a delicacy that reminds me of death.
So slender, each breath! She is hot
and the sweat glistens like ground glass
on her scalp. Her eyelids are almond petals,
white, exquisitely veined with pink.

Finer than her eyelashes are fine,
yet greater than the delta of the Nile,
are the rivulets of blood in the hoods
of her eyes. The mastery of her!
No human design can hide the design in her.
She holds me as I hold her while she is held
by sleep. Her eyelids flinch and flicker,
brushed by the bright blackness of dreams.

Darling, it seems they would have us believe
that, back beyond the generations, you
and I and they—we all—were spawned
spontaneously from an inorganic soup.
They say it is "scientific". But I know
it is unproven and unprovable, believable
only by faith. And it is a faith that fails
the facts. The facts, say, of your eyelids.

Child, I do not believe your eyelids
or the dreams above which they flutter
are accidental—a mere coincidence
of chemicals and light, a serendipity
of time and matter. I cannot believe.
I lack the faith. Daughter, dream this
true dream: Your spirit is the wick of Yahweh,
your body, the wax of His make and moulding.

Dream this waking and always. And burn
little candle! Burn brightly in the coming night!